N. Ginsberg

Burnout Busters

Stress Management For Ministry

Burnout Busters

Stress Management For Ministry

Joseph D. White, Ph.D.

Our Sunday Visitor Publishing Division
Our Sunday Visitor, Inc.
Huntington, Indiana 46750

Nihil Obstat:
Rev. Michael Heintz
Censor Librorum

Imprimatur:
✠ John M. D'Arcy
Bishop of Fort Wayne-South Bend
March 4, 2007

The *Nihil Obstat* and *Imprimatur* are declarations that a work is free from doctrinal or moral error. It is not implied that those who have granted the *Nihil Obstat* and *Imprimatur* agree with the contents, opinions, or statements expressed.

12 11 10 09 08 07 1 2 3 4 5 6 7 8 9

Our Sunday Visitor Publishing Division
Our Sunday Visitor, Inc.
200 Noll Plaza
Huntington, IN 46750

ISBN 978-1-59276-311-5 (Inventory No. X410)

Cover design by Amanda Miller
Interior design by Sherri L. Hoffman

Printed in the United States of America

Contents

INTRODUCTION

Burnout — Characteristics and Causes

Burnout — it may be difficult to define, but we know the signs that it's coming: the task list that repeats itself throughout a night of tossing and turning in bed; the dread of going into the office feeling like such a heavy weight that even getting dressed and ready for work in the morning seems to require extra effort; the pile of papers on the desk that gets so high it feels as if it will fall on us; the person who can't seem to leave us alone; the nagging desire to begin browsing the classified ads for something better — something different.

My wife and I sometimes joke that we are getting dangerously close to burnout when we unintentionally try to use our work key to open the front door at home!

Burnout is so common that nearly all of us have felt it at times, and it's especially common in ministry, for a number of reasons:

- The sheer importance of the work of ministry makes us want to work very hard at it, and we sometimes work harder or longer than we should.
- Because we live in an imperfect world, the work of ministry is never done. Ministry work will never be complete until the end of time.
- People often have unrealistic expectations of those involved in ministry work, seeing them as extraordinarily gifted or holy. This can be a double-edged sword. People expect more from those involved in ministry, and they react more negatively when ministers make a mistake.
- The persons to whom we are ministering may have very little insight into the various tasks that make up the minister's job. For example, they may assume that a religious-education director or

a member of the clergy really only works on Sundays and is relatively free the rest of the week.

- People who work in ministry are often working in the very communities they rely upon for social and spiritual support, and the dual relationships that result can pose complications for their work and personal lives.

These and other factors combine to make work in ministry a special challenge. But, of course, ministry has its benefits as well. Many who work in a ministry position find the work rewarding for many of the same reasons that sometimes cause stress — the importance of the work, the fact that there is always something new to do, and the helping relationships with people and the community work environment. Plus, as workers in God's vineyard, we are promised eternal reward in heaven, even when our jobs seem thankless at times here on earth. (Now *there's* a retirement plan!)

This short book is written especially for those who work in ministry. Whether you are a member of the clergy, a director of religious education, a volunteer catechist or teacher, parish social minister, diocesan employee, a Catholic school employee, youth minister, music minister, or one of countless other irreplaceable members of the Body of Christ, this book is for you. It combines spiritual and psychological principles to present a framework for preventing and managing stress in the unique environment of ministry.

As a clinical psychologist in diocesan ministry, I have often been asked to present workshops on this topic to a variety of ministry leaders and volunteers in the Church. This book draws upon some of what I have presented in these workshops, as well as what I have heard from those who have attended. It is my hope that you will find the suggestions offered here practical and relevant to the work you do. Along those lines, I encourage you to use this text as a workbook. Make it your own, customizing the material to your particular work and community as you see fit. Make notes as you go along. Write out your thoughts in response to the reflection questions, and if possible discuss them with others. Try the exercises that are suggested, but modify them to your particular needs. Let's begin this process now with some questions for reflection based on the points outlined above.

- What are some of the factors that cause stress (and could lead to burnout) in my work?

- What does burnout look like for me? How do I know when I am approaching burnout?

- What do I hope to gain from study of this text?

This book is written because *you* are important to the work of Christ. The Church needs you, and so you must make sure that in the selfless work of ministry you don't forget to care for yourself. If the minister does not allow himself or herself to be filled, refreshed, and at times, protected, there will be no one left to minister to others. Keep this in mind as you work through this text and as you go about your daily work. Next, we'll begin our discussion of preventing burnout by examining some ways to limit or prevent stress in our work.

PART ONE

Preventing Stress before It Occurs

CHAPTER ONE

"Know Thyself"

For we are [God's] workmanship, created in Jesus Christ for good works, which God prepared beforehand, that we should walk in them.
— EPHESIANS 2:10

A discussion of stress prevention really must start with the most fundamental question of human existence: "Who am I?" At the most basic level, there is one answer to this question that is true for all of us. "I am a physical and spiritual being created in the image of God." In the book of Genesis, we are told that human beings were created, male and female, in God's image. What does it mean to be created in God's image? Well, many books longer than this one could be written on that topic alone, but let's summarize by saying that to be created in God's image means to be created for loving, for we are told in Scripture that "God is love" (1 Jn 4:8). Jesus Christ, when asked about the greatest commandment, said, "You shall love the Lord your God with all your heart, and with all your soul, and with all your mind. This is the greatest and first commandment. And a second is like it, You shall love your neighbor as yourself. On these two commandments depend all the law and the prophets" (Mt 22:37–40).

Personality and Temperament

Pope John Paul II points out in his Theology of the Body that we are created as a unity of body and soul. Thus, we can't attend solely to the spiritual and ignore the physical; for what we do with our bodies, we also do with our souls. Physically, we are a product of our genetic endowment and the interaction of our genes with environmental factors, including nutrition, injury, physical exercise, and stress. Our mental and emotional selves are also formed by an interaction between genes and environment, but in a way that is more complex and less apparent to us. Scientific research has shown us that although personality develops over time as the individual matures and interacts with others, there are some traits that are observable even in infancy and early childhood and tend to remain stable over time. These traits include how outgoing or withdrawn we tend to be, how intensely we express ourselves, and how generally active or mellow we tend to be. These relatively stable traits combine to form what psychologists call temperament. Temperament may be thought of as the part of our personality that is inborn, or hard-wired in us.

In the book *The Temperament God Gave You*, Art Bennett, a licensed marriage and family therapist, and his wife, Laraine (2005), use an updated version of an ancient four-type model of temperament to discuss how individuals may have different interests, work styles, and ways of relating to one another depending on their particular temperament type.

> Whereas temperament should never be used as an excuse to avoid personal growth,
> if we recognize our temperamental assets and liabilities, we can identify what we will most likely be good at and what we might need some help with.

Those with a **choleric** temperament have a "take-charge" attitude. They are strong-willed and enthusiastic. They can have intense reactions, both positive and negative. They are rational and expect well-reasoned arguments from others.

The person with a **melancholic** temperament values the ideal. He or she reflects on things before making decisions. Compassion and thoughtfulness are common traits of the melancholic. He or she values the ideal and can be pious. An individual with a melancholic temperament may prefer to be alone at times, as he or she draws energy from solitude.

Those with a **sanguine** temperament are creative, fun-loving, and spirited. They love adventure and are quite outgoing. They tend to be optimistic and are big-picture dreamers. Those who are sanguine tend to be very passionate, and can have quick and intense emotional reactions.

Individuals with a **phlegmatic** temperament are reserved, prudent, sensible, and reflective. They tend to follow the rules, and enjoy tradition. They dislike confrontation and conflict. They are diplomatic and dependable, but can sometimes be accused of lacking enthusiasm or energy.

Our temperament type often has an impact on the career we choose, our strengths and weaknesses, and our relationships with others. Whereas temperament should never be used as an excuse to avoid personal growth, if we recognize our temperamental assets and liabilities, we can identify what we will most likely be good at and what we might need some help with. For example, when an individual with a sanguine temperament type gets a new idea, he or she may need a phlegmatic personality to discuss it with, looking for potential pitfalls and brainstorming on the detailed steps needed to reach the goal.

Temperament types may at times predispose us to some conflict. For example, individuals with choleric and sanguine temperaments are both enthusiastic and energetic, but one is more rational and one is more of a dreamer. Their differing perspectives, combined with their passion, may make for heated arguments.

QUESTIONS FOR REFLECTION

- Which of the four temperament types discussed in this chapter do I most closely identify with?

- What are some of the strengths and weaknesses associated with my temperament type?

Gifts and Talents

In addition to the strengths that may be associated with our temperament, God gives each of us other gifts and talents that can help make clear His plan for us. Three simple questions can help us identify some of those gifts and talents. Write your responses to the following:

- What do I really enjoy doing?

- What have I been successful at in the past?

- What things have other people told me I am good at?

We tend to be happiest when we are doing the things we were made to do — using our God-given talents and doing the things we enjoy. Sometimes, of course, we have a job we enjoy but there are aspects of our work that we are not as interested in (or talented at) as others. This will be discussed further in Chapter Four, titled "Know Thy Ministry."

Personal Mission Statement

For the past several years, mission statements have been an important part of corporate culture. A mission statement identifies the core beliefs and primary aims of the organization. More recently, there has been a great deal of discussion about one's "personal mission statement," a summary of an individual's own core beliefs and goals. Once we know something about our personalities and talents, we can draw upon this information in forming our own personal mission statement.

When we discuss the personal mission statement of an individual who is involved in ministry, it is helpful to examine the core beliefs of our faith and the overall mission of the Church. The core beliefs for Catholics and most Protestant Christians are summed up in the Apostles' Creed:

> I believe in God, the Father almighty,
> Creator of heaven and earth.
> I believe in Jesus Christ, his only Son, our Lord.
> He was conceived by the power of the Holy Spirit
> and born of the Virgin Mary.
> He suffered under Pontius Pilate,
> was crucified, died, and was buried.
> He descended into hell.
> On the third day he rose again.
> He ascended into heaven
> and is seated at the right hand of the Father.
> He will come again to judge the living and the dead.
> I believe in the Holy Spirit,
> the holy catholic Church,
> the communion of saints,
> the forgiveness of sins,
> the resurrection of the body,
> and the life everlasting.
> Amen.

The primary mission of the Church was given to us by Christ in the Great Commission:

"Go therefore and make disciples of all nations, baptizing them in the name of the Father and of the Son and of the Holy Spirit, teaching them to observe all that I have commanded you" (Mt 28:19).

The mission of the Church, then, is evangelization: sharing the Gospel with all. We can do this in many ways, of course. St. Francis once said, "Preach the Gospel at all times, and when necessary use words." Sharing the Good News of Christ is the task of all Christians, but we each do it in our own way, according to our own talents and abilities, as we are called by God. This may include acts of charity, work for social justice, teaching, preaching, writing, and countless other activities. In light of the core beliefs and primary mission of the Church, what is your personal mission statement? Reflect on this for a few moments, and write your thoughts below:

MY MISSION STATEMENT

My core beliefs:

My primary goal(s):

How I will carry out these goals:

CHAPTER TWO

Nurture Yourself Spiritually

For I delivered to you as of first
importance what I also received.
— 1 Cor 15:3

You then who teach others,
will you not teach yourself?
— Rom 2:21

In recent years, various studies have confirmed that paying attention to our spiritual lives helps to buffer us against stress. A Virginia Commonwealth University study published in the *American Journal of Psychiatry* (Kendler, 1997) found that people who are religious have less stress, a lower incidence of mental illness, and are less likely to abuse drugs and alcohol. Paying attention to our spiritual lives is good for our relationships as well. A 1999 study in the *Journal of Family Psychology* (Mahoney, et al., 1999) showed that an integration of religion and marriage "were consistently associated with greater global marital adjustment, more perceived benefits from marriage, decreased marital conflict, more verbal collaboration, and less use of verbal aggression and stalemate to discuss disagreements for both wives and husbands."

A well-developed spirituality is perhaps the most essential quality in a minister or ministry leader. Why? **Because we cannot hand on that which we do not have.** No matter what our particular ministry, we must first have a relationship with Christ in order to share Christ with others. Usually when we are in a close relationship with someone, we spend time together; we have frequent and intimate communication.

Although we may know Christ, we are never finished growing in our faith. The Christian life is a process of "continuing conversion." One way to help ensure that we continue to grow spiritually is to follow the pattern of the early Church, as seen in Acts:

> And they devoted themselves to the apostles' teaching and to fellowship, to the breaking of bread and the prayers (Acts 2:42).

For the early Christians, devotion to the apostles' teaching meant recognition of their unique authority in the life of the Church. This teaching authority followed from the special knowledge given to them by Jesus (see Lk 8:10), the power to bind and loose given by Christ to all the apostles and especially to Peter (Mt 18:18; 16:13–19), and the work of the Holy Spirit, given to the apostles by Jesus (Jn 20:22–23). The teaching authority of the apostles has been passed down through the generations through apostolic succession, and the teachings of the apostles are made known to us today in the Apostles' Creed and other essential teachings of the Church. "Devotion to the apostles' teaching" in modern times means a familiarity with Scripture and the *Catechism of the Catholic Church* and a trust in the Holy Spirit's ability to guide our Church as Jesus promised. So one way we can nourish ourselves spiritually is through study of Scripture and the *Catechism* and other writings that give us insights on the essential teachings of our faith.

A well-developed spirituality is perhaps the most essential quality in a minister or ministry leader.

Devotion to fellowship was another important, but sometimes overlooked, source of the strength for early Christians. They did many things together, and formed such a close-knit community that they were described as being of "one heart and soul" (Acts 4:32). It is vital to the life of the Church that Christians truly get to know one another and support one another. Our friends who are strong in the faith become important sources of counsel and guidance for us, and we for them. Forming this type of relationship takes both time and opportunities for informal interactions. Consider giving parish social events an important place on your family calendar. Invite other Christians to dinner. It is only when we spend time with one another and know one another well that we can "bear one another's burdens, and so fulfill the law of Christ" (Gal 6:2). Further discussion of social support is found in Chapter Three, "Maintain a Social Support Network."

For Christians today, devotion to "the breaking of bread" may be understood as immersion in the liturgical life of the Church, and the Eucharist in particular. Through the Eucharist, Christ becomes sacramentally present to us. Jesus himself nourishes us as we experience the power of His promise, "I am with you always" (Mt 28:20). The sacrament of reconciliation is another sacrament we have the privilege of celebrating on a regular basis, but how few of us regularly take advantage of this wonderful gift! Confession is simultaneously a reminder of God's unconditional love for us and an opportunity for us to let God heal those broken parts of our lives and mold us in His image. As we meet God in the sacraments, we experience grace — a share of God's own life. This grace gives us strength to minister to others and helps us to live as good examples.

Prayer has a rich and varied history in our faith tradition, from structured, meditative prayers such as the Rosary to spontaneous prayer, yet these diverse expressions are united in their goal to promote communication and intimacy with God. In addition to different prayer forms, we may wish to consider our use of various types of prayer. Prayers of praise tell God how wonderful He is. These prayers help us to remember God's place in our lives and foster our sense of wonder at His majesty and power. In prayers of supplication, we make our needs known to God. Following Jesus' example, we have the courage to approach God as His children — children of a loving Father who longs to meet our needs. Prayers of intercession enable us to bring the needs of others before God's throne. Our intercessions strengthen the Church by reminding us that we are one body and enabling us to share in one another's needs. Prayers of thanksgiving serve as our offering to God for the things He has given us and remind us of the many ways in which we are blessed. Finally, we must not overlook the act of listening in prayer. Speaking about prayer, Pope John Paul II once said, "When we hold a conversation with someone, we not only speak, but we also listen. Prayer, therefore, is also listening." We must take time to listen for the voice of God in our prayer and in our daily lives. God provides guidance when we listen for His voice.

SPIRITUAL GROWTH SELF-ASSESSMENT

- What nourishes me spiritually?

- How familiar am I with Scripture and the *Catechism*?

- What am I currently reading to help myself grow spiritually?

- In what ways do I participate in the liturgical life of the Church?

- When did I last celebrate the Sacrament of Reconciliation? How is God using this sacrament in my spiritual growth?

- Who is someone in my life who helps me grow spiritually?

- What am I doing right now to make connections with other Christians?

- What expressions and forms of prayer feel most natural to me? How can I further develop my prayer life?

CHAPTER THREE

Maintain a Social Support Network

Let us consider how to stir up one another to love and good works, not neglecting to meet together, as is the habit of some, but encouraging one another.
— Hebrews 10:24–25

Two decades ago, in a classic review of the psychological research on stress and coping, Drs. Sheldon Cohen and Tom A. Wills (1985) noted that social support protects individuals from the destructive effects of stress. They pointed out that both the perceived amount of support and the number of social contacts were important in this stress-buffering effect. Since that time, a number of studies have repeated this finding, some specific to stress in the work environment. In short, we know that the more support we have from others, the less burnout we are likely to feel, even if we work in potentially stressful jobs.

> Social support protects individuals from the destructive effects of stress.

For this reason, it is important even to our work itself to cultivate relationships with others. Times when hours are long and our work is intense are typically the times when we are spending the least time nurturing social relationships, but those times are precisely when we need the most support from others. For example, research has shown that most ethical breaches in the workplace occur around a decision made during a stressful time, but consultation with others is one of the best safeguards against unethical practices.

Here are some tips for nurturing our social support network, both within and outside the workplace:

- Take time out for lunch, and eat with coworkers. Research indicates that eating lunch at one's desk is one of the most reliable predictors of burnout.
- Look for ways to help others at work when they are overworked or overwhelmed. In St. Paul's teaching on the Body of Christ (1 Cor 12), we learn that collaboration is essential to the Church's functioning. Also, coworkers will be more willing to help us out in a bind if we have been considerate of them as well.
- When faced with a tough decision, especially in a stressful time, get input from others.
- If you are involved in parish ministry, seek out colleagues from other parishes who have similar positions to yours. This is good for consultation and collaboration (ideas can be shared), as well as venting about stressors and challenges, because we sometimes may not wish to vent to those we work with.
- If you are a diocesan priest or an individual in religious life who is living away from your community, look for others in a similar state and form a family of support in your area. Get together for "family meals" and other activities.
- Spend some time talking with coworkers about things other than work. Attend any social occasions such as office parties. On Mondays, ask about their weekends. Recommend good books, movies, and restaurants.
- Make time for connecting with family and friends. Schedule this time, if necessary. Vent about work some, if necessary, but be sure to set some limits on these discussions, or your loved ones may feel you are still mentally at work, rather than being present with them.
- Make "home time" home time. Leave work at work. We work more efficiently when we set limits on work time and environments. When at home, immerse yourself in the activities of family life. Do chores together with other family members, if possible (e.g., wash dishes together, fold clothes together, etc.).

- Have "family meals" together at a real table (not in front of a television)! Make this time sacred. When a family gathers around a table, they communicate better and more often.
- Try to find at least one extracurricular group to join. This might be a group that shares a particular hobby, a reading group at the local library, or just a group of friends who gets together on a regular basis for movies, cards, quilting, golf, or similar activities.
- Take your days off, don't accumulate vacation time you will never use, and have a day of rest at least one day per week (even if it can't be Sunday).

When we connect with others, we live happier, healthier lives and we perform better in the workplace. Using the questions below as a guide, reflect on the good things you are doing right now to cultivate a network of support, and consider some of things you might wish to do in the future.

QUESTIONS FOR REFLECTION

- When do I feel most supported by others?

- Who are the people I turn to for support? Why?

- What good things am I doing right now to maintain a social support network?

- What new things can I do to increase my network of support?

CHAPTER FOUR

"Know Thy Ministry"

Whatever your task, work heartily,
as serving the Lord.
— COLOSSIANS 3:23

To be content with our work in ministry, it's important that we have a clear sense of purpose — a calling to do that which we do and an understanding of exactly what the task involves. Perhaps this sounds obvious, but knowing our ministry may involve several different dimensions. For example:

- There may be specific guidelines regarding this ministry that come from the Vatican, the national body of bishops, or your national professional organization (e.g., NCCL, NCEA, etc.). For example, a catechist or catechetical leader should be familiar with the General and National Directories for Catechesis, and a director of liturgy should know the key points in the General Instruction for the Roman Missal and other liturgical documents.
- A diocese may have local guidelines or policies regarding certain ministries. For example, dioceses often have guidelines for preparation for and celebration of the Sacrament of Matrimony.
- A parish, school, or organization may have a mission statement that (hopefully) incorporates the particular ministry. There may also be specific policies for the ministry (e.g., sacramental guidelines).
- A particular position (even a volunteer one) should have a job description that details the purposes of the position and the specific tasks involved. If your position does not have a job description, ask your supervisor if you can work together on one.

As you reflect on your particular responsibilities, it's helpful to have a summary to which you can refer. To this end, fill in the form below (or use a separate sheet of paper if necessary).

GUIDELINES FOR MY MINISTRY

Vatican guidelines (official worldwide Church documents that provide directives for this ministry):

National guidelines for this ministry (any directives for this ministry from the United States Conference of Catholic Bishops):

Diocesan policies regarding this ministry:

Parish, school, or organizational policies regarding this ministry (What is the overall mission statement, and how does this work fit within that mission? What school or parish-wide policies exist regarding this ministry?):

Job description of my specific role in this ministry:

To be content with our work in ministry, it's important that we have a clear sense of purpose — a calling to do that which we do and an understanding of exactly what the task involves.

Once you are familiar with the mission, goals, objectives, and policies for your position, you will hopefully see some overlap between what you are doing and the personal mission statement you drafted in Chapter One.

Of course, you may find that your position in ministry is generally consistent with what you feel called to do, yet certain parts of your work involve things you would rather not do. For example, in my work as a psychologist, it is important that I do a great deal of record keeping. Keeping timely and thorough records is neither a talent nor an interest of mine, but in order to keep doing what I enjoy and am best at (counseling individuals and families), I have been challenged to develop my skills in this area.

Likewise, your position in ministry may involve some tasks at which you are not particularly skilled. This probably does not mean you should change jobs, but you may be facing a need to develop new competencies. When you identify a skill at which you need to grow, here are a few potential remedies to consider:

- Ask someone who has this skill to mentor you.
- Identify self-study courses using books or the Internet.
- Take a continuing-education workshop or class in this area.
- Identify modifications to your work that would compensate for this deficiency.
- Discuss the expectations for your position with a supervisor and determine whether your job description could be modified to better suit your interests and skills.

The key is to work toward, as close as possible, a correlation between your "personal mission," your talents and skills, and your job description. The more you are doing the things you really feel called to do and the things you are good at, the better you will feel about your work and the less likely you will be to experience burnout. Take a few moments now to reflect upon the guidelines for your work and how they relate to your interests and skills. Write your thoughts in the spaces below.

- Ways in which my current position fits my interest and skills:

- Current responsibilities that do not fit my personal mission, my interests, and/or my skills:

- Potential strategies for creating a better match of responsibilities, mission, interests, and skills:

CHAPTER FIVE

Practice Healthy Habits

Do you not know that your body is a temple of the Holy Spirit within you, which you have from God? You are not your own; you were bought with a price. So glorify God in your body.
— 1 Corinthians 6:19–20

As was mentioned earlier in this book, we are a unity of body and soul. We could extend this to say that our body, soul, mind, and emotions are all interrelated. When we are under severe stress, our bodies may respond with muscle tension, digestive problems, headaches, and a general lowering of immune functioning. Likewise, when we are physically very ill, we have little mental or emotional energy. Because of this close relationship between our physical, emotional, and mental selves, if we wish to avoid emotional or mental stress, we should take care of our bodies.

Eat a Balanced Diet

One important way to care for our bodies is by eating a balanced diet. The United States Department of Agriculture (USDA) has developed a pyramid model of healthy eating that consists of five basic food groups. The USDA recommends the following for a balanced diet:

- Most individuals should have about three ounces daily of whole grain bread, cereal, crackers, rice, or pasta.
- Eat more vegetables — especially dark green and orange vegetables and dry beans and peas.
- Eat a variety of fruits, whether fresh, frozen, canned, or dried. Go easy on fruit juices, which may contain a great deal of added sugar and do not have all the nutritional benefits of whole fruit.

- Consume low fat or fat-free milk and dairy products. If you are lactose intolerant, try lactose-free dairy products or be sure to look for other sources of calcium.
- Eat lean meats and poultry, broiled, baked, or grilled (rather than fried). Vary your choices, with more fish, beans, peas, nuts, and seeds as protein sources.

In addition, many nutritionists recommend eating fewer calories later in the day, when you won't really have a chance to burn them off. Eat a hearty breakfast, a balanced lunch, and a light dinner (before 7 P.M., if possible). Avoid sugary snacks, and limit the number of meals eaten out. Many restaurant meals are higher in calories, especially fast-food meals. If you must eat out, ask for smaller portions, or half your meal before you begin eating, saving the other half for tomorrow's lunch. Drink water when possible, as sodas and other sugar drinks add unnecessary calories.

For more information about a healthy diet, including a customized food pyramid for your age, gender, and amount of physical activity, see www.mypyramid.gov.

> There is a strong relationship between lack of adequate sleep and depression, anxiety, and other emotional problems.

Get Plenty of Rest

According to sleep researchers, the average adult needs about eight hours of sleep per night (yes, it's still true!). However, Americans are getting less and less sleep, and the sleep we get is often not as restful as it could be. This affects our efficiency on the job (our speed, ability to focus, and other factors) as well as our mood. There is a strong relationship between lack of adequate sleep and depression, anxiety, and other emotional problems. If you are currently not getting enough sleep or not getting restful sleep, consider the following tips:

- Turn off all electronics, including computers, TV, etc., at least an hour or two before you plan to go to sleep. This will give your mind a chance to calm down from the stimulation of modern technology.

- Consider your "sleep hygiene" — your bedtime rituals and the environment in which you sleep. Try to have an established, relaxing routine prior to going to bed — perhaps a warm bath, or the like. Make sure your bedding is sufficiently comfortable.
- Avoid doing other activities like working, watching TV, or reading in bed. Your body may begin to associate bed with these activities instead of with sleep. If you lay in bed for some time without falling asleep, get up, go somewhere else, and read until you feel sleepy.
- Buy heavier drapes, shades, or an eye mask if too much light is getting into the room at night.
- Keep your sleep schedule fairly consistent, even on weekends. Sleeping late on the weekends does not really help us catch up on sleep lost during the week, and may actually make us more tired, according to sleep experts.
- If you suspect you might have a sleep disorder, such as sleep apnea or restless leg syndrome, talk with your doctor about it. Many medical advances have been made in dealing with common sleep problems.

Remember to Exercise

There are numerous benefits to regular exercise. One is its power to combat stress. Vigorous exercise releases natural stress-fighting chemicals, called endorphins, in the brain. In addition to exercise keeping stress away, some studies have shown both regular aerobic exercise and weight lifting to be comparable in their effects to treatment with antidepressant medication. A brisk walk, bike ride, or swim are all great ways to exercise.

If you are unable to exercise daily, try a half-hour three or four times a week. Also, consider small ways in which you can increase your physical activity. For example, when running errands (e.g., at the mall or grocery store), park farther away from the door to increase walking time. Walk up stairs instead of using the elevator, and walk or bike rather than drive when traveling short distances.

QUESTIONS FOR REFLECTION

1. What kinds of foods should I add to my diet? What should I eat or drink less of?

2. How much sleep am I currently getting? Do I feel rested in the morning? (If not, what can I try to improve this situation?)

3. How can I work more physical activity into my daily routine?

CHAPTER SIX

Get Organized!

Everything must be done
properly and in order.
— 1 Corinthians 14:40 (NAB)

Does your desk look like a mountain of papers, or worse yet, like the Leaning Tower of Pisa? Do you sometimes lose phone messages before you've had a chance to return them? Is your e-mail inbox so littered with messages that you sometimes miss important messages or forget which messages you have answered and which ones you haven't? If you answered "yes" to any of these questions, this chapter is for you.

Organization is essential to working efficiently and preventing stress, but it's precisely at those times when we are busiest that we often find ourselves the least organized. Following are some pointers for getting — and staying — organized.

Desk

Your desk may or may not be where you are when you are actively ministering to others, but it is likely the "home base" or "organizational center" of your ministry. It should be clear enough to provide you a place to work, free of distractions and teetering piles of books and paper. If your desk is covered right now, block off a substantial amount of time, take everything off your desk, and put it in one stack on the floor. Now, sort that pile into smaller stacks according to topic (for example, "bills to pay," "things to order," "correspondence to answer," etc.). You may also wish to have a stack labeled "ASAP" for items that need your attention in the next 48 hours or so. Throw away anything you can (being realistic about what you will actually need or use in the future).

Any stacks to which you will need to attend weekly should be put into standing files on your desk. Buy a desktop vertical file frame from an office supply store, and get sturdy cardboard or plastic file folders to go in it. Label each folder and put the folders in the standing frame. Put the stacks of paper into the folders according to the labels you have created. Now, you can see all the papers you will need to attend to, and they take up less space on your desk. As you work throughout the week, make sure no one folder gets too full before you've had a chance to go through it. When you do sort through it, make a decision about every piece of paper so that you don't find yourself reviewing the same things over and over. You might wish to have a desktop "tickler" file for something you want to remind yourself to look at in one month. Review this folder on the same day each month. (Put it on your calendar!)

> With a little organization and efficient communication, one can dramatically reduce both wasted time and unnecessary stress.

Papers that you want to save for reference at a later date should be archived in an easily accessible filing cabinet, unless you know when you will need them. Your file cabinet may have quarterly or six-month tickler files (or even a file for each month of the year) for things you want to remind yourself about in the future. Other folders should be labeled and organized according to topic. Make sure the folders in your filing cabinet don't get cluttered with outdated items or things you are unlikely to use. Periodically throw out these items so that you will be able to keep your files current.

Make sure your desk doesn't get too cluttered with office supplies. Keep the basics on hand — stapler, tape, scissors, pens, paper clips, and so on — and put the rest in a drawer or rolling caddy next to the desk.

Now your "home base" is clear, and you are ready to work efficiently. You will need to repeat this process periodically. Build time into your schedule for maintaining this system of organization. Investing a little time on a regular basis will save you the time you might have spent finding lost items or becoming distracted by clutter. When mail comes in each day, make a decision about each piece of mail as you sort through it. Should it go in the trash? Should it be filed? If so, where?

Phone

Phone messages can also overwhelm us at times. Office supply stores sell spiral-bound phone logs that have space for the time and date of the call, the person who called, the phone number, and notes about the message. Some also have a box to check when the call is returned. Purchase one of these message logs, and write all phone messages down in one place when you are checking your voice mail. If you have an assistant who takes messages for you, have him or her write messages down in a log as well. As you return the calls, make a note of this, writing the date and time you returned the call and noting whether you left a message, got a busy signal, or made contact. You might wish to prioritize messages on a daily basis based on the urgency of the call, but don't put off returning messages so long that you lose track of an unreturned message on a previous page of your log.

On your outgoing voice-mail message, provide as much information as possible, and ask callers to leave a detailed message, including their name, number, and the reason for their call. If you get a voice mailbox instead of a live person when you return phone messages, be sure to leave a detailed response. It is sometimes possible to respond to questions or provide the information an individual was seeking without actually having a conversation. This will save time that would otherwise have been wasted playing "phone tag." Be sure to document your attempts to return calls, whether or not you are able to make contact. If you attempt to call back once or twice and are not able to reach the individual, give the person another chance to call you.

When you do make contact, keep phone calls brief, staying on topic, and setting limits with the caller if necessary. Ronni Eisenberg and Kate Kelly (1997), authors of *Organize Yourself!*, recommend warning callers in advance that you have a limited amount of time (e.g., "I have about five minutes; can you tell me about your concern briefly?"). They also recommend inserting "before we hang up" as a warning to the other person that you must end the call soon, and keeping a clock or timer next to the phone to remind you not to let the time slip away.

E-mail

E-mail can be an efficient and satisfying way in which to communicate, provided that it is used well. There aren't any busy signals with e-mail, and conversations can be kept brief when necessary. Here are some tips for keeping e-mail communications effective and organized:

- Purchase a good "spam" filter that will block unwanted bulk e-mails.
- Build time to review and respond to e-mails into your daily schedule.
- Most e-mail programs will allow you to create folders in your e-mail. Make use of this feature and categorize items in a manner similar to the desktop files recommended earlier.
- Respond to e-mails you plan to respond to, and delete or file them right away. Don't leave them in your inbox unnecessarily.
- Be aware that e-mail communication is unique in the sense that it is lacking the context clues of phone and in-person conversations (e.g., tone of voice, facial expressions). If your messages or responses are short and sweet, make sure they don't sound overly curt or rude.

With a little organization and efficient communication, one can dramatically reduce both wasted time and unnecessary stress. If a total organization makeover is too much to manage right now, consider taking it in small steps. Make a little time each day to organize the desk, then tackle the e-mail, and then change the system for phone messages.

QUESTIONS FOR REFLECTION

1. What am I already doing to stay organized? What's working best?

2. What new habits or techniques can I try?

CHAPTER SEVEN

Know When to Say "No"

"Let your 'Yes' mean 'Yes,'
and your 'No' mean 'No.'"
— MATTHEW 5:37 (NAB)

Perhaps the most difficult part of working in ministry is learning when to say "No," where to set our limits, or how to say, "I just need a break right now." This is because ministry work is typically done by people who are naturally very giving, and because they are working for God and for others, it feels selfish to say "No." But trying to meet everyone's needs all the time, feeling like we must say "Yes" to every good idea, or doing something just because no one else will is a surefire path to burnout. Forty hours a week is considered full time for a reason; the more we work past forty to fifty hours, the less efficient we get, meaning that we might work 55 hours and not actually get more work done than if we had worked 45. The key is to prioritize, to set limits, and thereby work efficiently.

So how do we know when to say "No" and how do we do it? The first step is to prioritize our work. Look back at the job description you wrote for yourself in Chapter Four. Of all the responsibilities you have, which are the most important? Which are the most urgent? These may be two separate categories, but both very important and very urgent tasks should be prioritized. Using the following list, rank the primary responsibilities of your position, with urgent and important tasks at the top of the list, and less urgent or important tasks at the bottom.

MY PRIORITIES

1.

2.

3.

4.

5.

6.

The way in which these priorities are ranked may change, depending on the project you are working on or the current issues associated with your ministry. Therefore, this list of priorities may be more aptly called "My Job Description Right Now."

Each possible task or request should be compared with your list of priorities to determine which tasks come first each day (or each week). When you make your list of things to do, rank each item based on its priority, and then complete them in order of priority. This is crucial; we often find ourselves feeling stressed because we did the easy things on the list first, and spent too much time on them, neglecting other things that were very important or urgent. Estimate the time that will be spent on each task and build room for this in your schedule. If there isn't time for everything, you may have to sacrifice the items at the bottom of your list.

Now imagine that another task, request, or opportunity comes your way. If you work in a parish, perhaps it is a parishioner who says, "We ought to have ____________ at this parish. That would fall under your ministry, right?" Or maybe it is an invitation to be part of a committee, or to lead in another ministry area. Because you have spent some time reflecting on your personal and ministry mission, your job description, and your current priorities, you can screen this request or opportunity using the following questions:

- Does it fit the organizational mission statement?
- Does it fit my own role/job description within the organization?
- Does it fit with my current priorities on the job?
- Does it take time and energy away from other good things?

There may be times when our own job description needs to be expanded, or when, in the interest of collaboration, we lend a hand with something for which someone else is most directly responsible. However, we can't do this at the expense of more urgent or important tasks.

Saying "No" to a Good Idea

When people bring a new idea (or something they think is new) to you, they are most likely doing so partly because they want you to try what they are suggesting, and partly because they are seeking affirmation. They want to be helpful to others and thought of as such. Faced with an often large number of good ideas, but limited time, we might have to say "No" to the implementation, but we can still give affirmation. Our response might go something like this:

"I think your idea is great. I really wish I could do it, but right now my plate is full."

If the idea really is something you might like to try in the future, you may wish to add something like this:

"Perhaps we'll be in a place where we can try this in six months or so. Can you be sure to remind me then so that we can consider it again?"

Saying "No" to a Bad Idea

Sometimes individuals ask us to do something we're fairly sure would not be the best course of action. We can kindly decline in a number of ways, depending on why we feel the suggestion or request is problematic. If we want to say "No" because we have tried something before, we need to remember to include some affirmation in our response:

"You and I think alike. I thought that would be helpful, too, and tried it last year. If we were going to do something like that again, we would need to understand better why it didn't work the first time, and do it differently."

Or, if the idea or request doesn't work for other reasons, we can provide affirmation for the individual's intentions:

"I can understand why you would want this done. I can tell that you really have the (parish's/school's/organization's) good in mind."

And then plainly state why you would need to decline:

"Unfortunately, this doesn't fit with our mission statement right now," or, "I'm afraid we wouldn't be able to do this, because we have a (school/diocesan/parish/organizational) policy that says. . . ."

When the Request Comes from the Top: Saying "No" to Your Supervisor

We may often feel that when we are asked to do something by our supervisor, we must comply. But if you work for someone with real vision, they might sometimes come up with a number of great ideas that need further thought, or they might be unaware that they have assigned us more than we can handle. At those times, we can respond like this:

"I really like this idea in theory, but I can see a few potential problems we might need to work out before we do it," or, "This sounds great, but right now I'm spending most of my time on _________. Do you want me to continue to prioritize those things, or should I stop doing one of those things so that I can work this in?"

Or, if there is an organizational policy that the supervisor is not considering: "I can understand why you would want to do that, but don't our policies say (state policy)?"

Deferring Tasks When Necessary

There might be times when we are presented with good ideas or requests that either don't fall under our specific roles or are not things we can take on personally, but may be important enough that we want them to happen, if possible. At these times, we might need to say:

"I'm glad to hear your idea," or, "I understand what you're asking," and then, "Let me tell you whom you would need to talk with about that."

Or if the idea falls under our specific role, but we can't do it personally, try the following:

"That sounds great. I would need someone who could take responsibility for this, though. Are you willing to take this on?"

Delegating Responsibilities

Another way to get important things done when we can't do them personally is to delegate. People to whom you might delegate tasks could include employees or volunteers you currently supervise or an advisory board you have created for your area of ministry. Also, you might decide that it is time for a very large-scale delegation of tasks that requires a larger pool of participants.

When my wife and I worked together as directors of faith formation in a large parish, we realized over time that we were attempting to do much, much more than we could do on our own. Looking first at the Church's documents on catechesis, we observed the Church's firm teaching that parents have first and primary responsibility for teaching the faith to their children. With our pastor's support, we decided to require parent participation in the program as a prerequisite to registration. We developed a multitude of volunteer job descriptions, including: catechists, catechist's assistants, prayer team members (who committed to one hour of prayer each week for the needs of faith formation in our parish), a special events team (to help us with liturgical year celebrations and similar occasions), an arts and crafts team (who helped us with craft projects in the catechetical sessions), and other positions that fit the needs of our particular parish. Parents who already served in other ministries were asked to be a "parish ministry liaison," which involved a commitment to speaking once or twice with our religious education students about their ministry and what it involves. For example, extraordinary ministers of Holy Communion visited our second-grade sessions to teach them the proper way to receive the Eucharist. Choir members and other musicians shared their gift of song with the group.

Adults who were already a part of a faith-formation session during their children's class sessions or who were interested in doing so were also told that they were making a huge contribution to their children's faith development by working to grow in their own faith, so attendance at adult faith-formation sessions was considered a fulfillment of the requirement. (Incidentally, this boosted our participation in adult faith formation and also gave us a great pool of future catechists. When adults begin to grow in their faith, they naturally want to share it with others.)

An important lesson we learned from this is that the volunteers we need are probably out there, but either haven't been called by us in the right ways or haven't been given a sufficient variety of specific ways to serve.

You might be concerned about asking for such a wide-scale volunteer commitment, feeling that people will balk at this request. We were concerned about this as well, but interestingly, out of 820 children that were enrolled in our program, only two parents complained about the new requirement that all parents be involved in the ministry. Many of the other parents thanked us profusely for providing so many potential ways to be involved. An important lesson we learned from this is that the volunteers we need are probably out there, but either haven't been called by us in the right ways or haven't been given a sufficient variety of specific ways to serve.

Another concern about delegation of responsibility is that it increases our own responsibilities in some ways. We have more people to supervise, and must invest time in coordinating our volunteers. But stay away from the temptation to say, "I can do it easier myself." The Church is, by design, a collaborative group of individuals serving together. Keep working on a system that allows you to work effectively with your volunteers, and you will eventually find that you have more time, not less.

QUESTIONS FOR REFLECTION

1. What do I need to say "No" to right now? How will I do this?

2. What current responsibilities do I have that can be deferred or delegated? What is my plan of action for accomplishing this?

PART TWO

Managing the Stress That Is Already Present

CHAPTER EIGHT

Know the Basic Principles of Stress Management

Anxiety in a man's heart weighs him down.
— PROVERBS 12:25

The basic principles of stress management are well summarized in the "Serenity Prayer," made famous by Alcoholics Anonymous:

> God, grant me the serenity to accept the things I cannot change, courage to change the things I can, and the wisdom to know the difference.

The basic principles of stress management, the keys to coping with stress, are:

- Accept the things you cannot change.
- Change the things you can.
- Learn to know the difference.

Much of the stress we face in everyday life comes from trying to change the unchangeable or from not taking steps to correct problems we can solve. When we learn to know the difference, we can apply the appropriate coping skills — strategies to effectively manage stress.

Emotion-focused coping is the name psychologists give to a variety of skills aimed at accepting what we cannot change. Emotion-focused coping involves changing how we think about a situation or using relaxation techniques to help ourselves feel better. **When we use emotion-focused coping, the situation itself does not change, but we change our reaction to it.** Emotion-focused coping is effective for stressful events we have to endure because we are working toward a greater goal (e.g., academic stress in the course of earning a degree, enduring a painful medical procedure that is medically necessary, or managing the stress of day-to-day activities [or hectic times of year] in a job that we otherwise enjoy). Emotion-focused coping is also useful for dealing with situations that, after careful consideration, we realize are completely beyond our control — situations that depend on people or events we have little influence over.

> Much of the stress we face in everyday life comes from trying to change the unchangeable or from not taking steps to correct problems we can solve.

Problem-focused coping involves tackling the situation head-on in a structured, organized way. **When we use problem-focused coping, we change the situation that is causing us stress.** When we carefully consider a stressful situation and realize that we have some control over the situation itself, not just our reaction to it, we can implement problem-focused strategies to lessen the stress or to resolve the situation all together. Problem-focused strategies are good for dealing with variables that mostly depend on our own actions, or on the actions of people over whom we have some influence.

Some situations may involve aspects over which we have control and variables that are beyond our control. For example, if we are planning a large outdoor event, we have some control over organizing the event itself and having a contingency plan in case of bad weather, but the weather itself is beyond our control. In these situations, we must determine what we have some control over and take responsibility for that, while accepting and coping with the things we cannot change. We then might employ both emotion-focused and problem-focused techniques.

The next four chapters discuss strategies for emotion-focused and problem-focused coping. Prior to reading through these chapters, consider the stressors you are currently facing in your ministry (or ones you anticipate), and categorize them in the following chart.

CURRENT STRESSORS IN MY MINISTRY WORK

Things over which I have some control (use problem-focused coping for these items):

Things that are beyond my control (use emotion-focused coping for these items):

CHAPTER NINE

Emotion-Focused Coping, Part One: Think Helpful Thoughts

For as he thinks within himself, so he is.
— PROVERBS 23:7 (NASB)

The effects of positive thinking were first studied scientifically when it was observed that individuals in very similar or even identical situations sometimes reacted very differently. Viktor Frankl (2006), a psychologist and Holocaust survivor, observed that positive thinking, even in the face of unimaginable brutality, was essential to survival of the concentration camps. Psychologists investigating the long-term effects of serious losses, abuse, and neglect in childhood have observed similar differences in outcomes based on how individuals ultimately make sense of negative events and what impact these events have on their thinking.

Psychologist Roy Baumeister and colleagues (1990) studied how individuals may see the same situations very differently depending on the perspective they take. In one study on interpersonal conflict, they asked participants to write about the same event from multiple sides, first as the person who was hurt by the actions of another, and then as the person who was being hurtful. Interestingly, even the factual details of the story changed quite a bit depending on the perspective they were taking. For example, the different accounts written by the same person showed differences in time spans and in the severity of the events themselves.

All this goes to show that we do not necessarily see the world as it is, we see the world as we are. We look at life though our own set of glasses, rose-colored or otherwise! There are often multiple ways of looking at the same situation that are all technically factual. We might see the glass as half empty or half full. We might see a difficult situation as an obstacle or as a challenging opportunity. What we need to do is to begin to pay attention to what is the most helpful way to look at the situation — what helps me accomplish what I need to accomplish — to work through the difficult times (or at least cope with them). Our thoughts are closely related to our feelings. If we are thinking about things in unhelpful, negative ways, we will feel bad, sometimes unnecessarily.

When we are familiar with the common types of negative or unhelpful thinking, we can begin to catch ourselves when we are viewing situations in unhelpful ways, and we can begin to take a more helpful perspective. Here are some common types of unhelpful thinking:

- **Expecting the worst.** When we expect something bad to happen, we can sometimes inadvertently turn our thoughts into self-fulfilling prophecies. We have to allow for the possibility, or even the probability, that things will go well.
- **Shifting the blame.** This occurs when we fail to take responsibility for things we could have done differently, or when we blame ourselves for things that aren't our fault. This kind of thinking is unhelpful because it keeps us from finding real solutions to our problems.
- **Perfectionistic thinking / exaggerating little things.** This type of thinking occurs when we make small problems bigger than they are, and we let small details that don't go well ruin whole days, projects, or events. Very few things in life are perfect, and we must learn to cope with small imperfections in ourselves and in the world around us.
- **Minimizing or discounting the positive.** If things have been going wrong and circumstances take a turn for the better, we might tend to mistrust the good things that are happening and find some other (possibly far-fetched) explanation for them. We won't let good things be good, and consequently, we still feel frustrated or sad.
- **Labeling.** People tend to live up to their reputations, and when we call ourselves or other people names in response to negative

Our thoughts are closely related to our feelings. If we are thinking about things in unhelpful, negative ways, we will feel bad, sometimes unnecessarily.

events, we can make what might have been a onetime occurrence a pattern of behavior. Don't call yourself a loser unless you're determined to be one all the time!

- **Absolute thinking.** This type of thinking is extreme. It involves looking at things as all one way or all another. For example, if something isn't going right for us on the job, we might decide we don't like anything about our work. An individual might be either be all wonderful in our eyes or all bad. But the world rarely works that way. Many events, people, and environments are a mixture of things we like or agree with and things we don't. If we engage in absolute thinking, we will miss important information that could help us feel better or work more effectively.
- **Denial.** Positive thinking doesn't mean ignoring problems when they are present. Ignoring something that's going wrong can make a small problem much bigger.

Here are some practical examples of how we might rephrase unhelpful thoughts and make them more helpful to us:

Instead of:	*Try:*
I think this will be a bad day.	I'm hoping for the best.
It's all his fault.	We all bear some responsibility here. How can we make this better?
This ruins my whole project!	I've identified a challenge that I need to work on.
I wonder why he is being nice to me? He must want something.	He's being nice to me. This is a refreshing change.
I'm a loser.	I made a mistake, but I'll do it differently next time.
There is nothing good about her.	She has good and bad qualities, just like everyone else.
Everything is fine. I can't think about what's going wrong.	I need to address some problems before they get bigger.

Positive thinking is a powerful tool that can assist us in many stressful circumstances. What are some of the unhelpful thoughts you sometimes have? How can you begin to think more positively about these issues? Use the following space to show how you will begin to transform your thinking.

Unhelpful thought:	*A more helpful alternative:*
1.	1.
2.	2.
3.	3.
4.	4.
5.	5.

CHAPTER TEN

Emotion-Focused Coping, Part Two: Practice Relaxation Skills

"Be still, and know that I am God."
— Psalm 46:10

As previously mentioned, stress can be stored up in our bodies as muscle tension, resulting in aches and pains. The opposite is also true. The more relaxed our bodies are, the less stressed we feel. Calming the body can calm our minds and our emotions.

Deep Breathing: The Foundation of Relaxation

A first step to practicing relaxation as an emotion-focused coping skill is remembering how to breathe. I say remembering because infants and small children do this naturally. They take slow, deep, full breaths. As adults, we forget how to breathe, and tend to take shallow, faster breaths, especially when we are stressed. A good metaphor to visualize as you practice deep breathing is a clear glass being filled with water. The water goes to the bottom of the glass, and the water level then rises. When we take nice, full breaths, we should be conscious of our breath going to the bottom of our lungs first, and then filling the rest of the lungs. Try this step-by-step approach:

- Put one hand over your belly.
- Inhale slowly and deeply through your nose only. Your belly should come out as you inhale, and then the rest of your lungs should fill with air.
- Exhale through your nose and mouth.

Note that we do not need to move our shoulders to take a full, deep breath. Keep your shoulders relaxed as you breathe.

Try five slow, deep breaths, and note how you feel afterward.

Progressive Relaxation Training

Progressive relaxation training (PRT) is another, even more powerful way to relax that combines the deep breathing you just practiced with muscle relaxation. In this approach, various muscles are tensed and held for a few seconds, and then relaxed. You might ask, "Why would we tense our muscles in order to relax?" Because purposeful tensing of muscle groups can fatigue the muscles and force them to relax. An important rule to keep in mind when practicing this technique is never tense a muscle to the point of pain. You should feel a real difference between tensing and relaxing, but these exercises shouldn't hurt. If you have had chronic pain in one or more muscle groups, be sure to consult with your doctor before attempting these exercises.

> These exercises should take ten minutes or less, but for most people, the payoff from doing them regularly is enormous.

The following steps are adapted from a technique developed by Drs. Steven Auerbach and Sandra Gramling (1997), two psychologists who work with medical professionals on behavioral ways to reduce stress and manage chronic pain. You'll want to be seated in a straight-backed chair as you complete these exercises. As you tense each muscle group, inhale fully and deeply. Exhale as you relax the muscles. Perform each step twice before proceeding to the next step.

1. Arch your eyebrows as high as they will go, wrinkling your forehead muscles. Hold them for a few seconds, and then relax.
2. Tense the muscles around your eyes and nose by closing your eyes tightly and crinkling up the nose (as if someone has just opened a jar of something that smells terrible right in front of your nose). Hold for a few seconds, and then relax as you exhale.
3. Tense the muscles of the mouth, jaw, and front of the neck by biting down gently on your back teeth, and then drawing down the corners of the mouth into an exaggerated frown like mimes do. You will feel your neck muscles tense if you do this correctly. Hold, and then relax and exhale.

4. Tense the muscles in the back of the neck by drawing the chin into the Adam's apple. Hold for a few seconds and relax while exhaling.
5. Tense the shoulders and top of the back by taking a slow, deep breath while pulling the shoulder blades back, arching the back, and attempting to touch your elbows together behind you. (I haven't met anyone who could make their elbows touch, but trying to do this will tense the right muscles.) After a few seconds, relax and exhale.
6. Tense the upper arms by pushing your elbows gently into the back of the chair behind you. You should feel your upper arm muscles tense up as you do this. After a few seconds, relax and exhale.
7. Tense the hands and lower arm muscles by making a fist with your thumbs on the outside of the fist, and squeezing your hands tightly as if there is a lemon in each hand and you are trying to squeeze out every drop of juice.
8. Tense your legs by lifting them up off the floor straight in front of you as you inhale. Attempt to point your toes out in front of you as well. Hold for a few seconds, and relax as you exhale.
9. Finally, lift your legs straight out again, but this time point your toes back toward you. You should feel tension in your calves as you do this. Relax and exhale.

When done correctly, these exercises should take ten minutes or less, but for most people, the payoff from doing them regularly is enormous.

Visualization

Closing one's eyes and picturing a calm and peaceful place, a favorite vacation destination, a happy time, or something similar, can also be an effective way to relax and escape for a few minutes when we need to. Take a few minutes to picture a peaceful place or a calming memory. Write the details of your mental picture here:

MY PEACEFUL PLACE

Location/occasion:

Things I see:

Things I hear:

Things I feel:

Things I smell:

Other people who are there (if any):

Find a quiet place to sit or lie down, close your eyes, take a few deep breaths, and try to picture yourself in this safe place. Spend a few minutes here, and try to carry that feeling of peace back with you to your current environment.

Practice Makes Perfect

Try to practice relaxation at least once or twice per day and more often, if necessary, when things become very hectic. These simple exercises take little time and can be done practically anywhere.

CHAPTER ELEVEN

Problem-Focused Coping, Part One: Solve Problems Effectively

"I, wisdom, dwell in prudence, and I find knowledge and discretion."
— Proverbs 8:12

The term executive functioning refers to the process by which we pay attention to important details, make decisions about what we perceive, determine possible alternatives, act on those alternatives and evaluate the results. Executive functioning takes place in the cerebral cortex, the highest level of the brain, specifically a part of the brain called the "frontal lobe." The emotional center of the brain, the limbic system, is where we experience emotions. When we are highly stressed, the limbic system is activated, and activity in the frontal lobes lessens. Put simply, we don't do our best problem-solving when we are feeling very emotional.

There is a step-by-step process we go through when we encounter ordinary problems in the course of daily life. For example, if I was going outside to run some errands and noticed my car was looking lopsided, I would make some closer observations and perhaps discover I had a flat tire. I would then consider some alternative courses of action (e.g., find other transportation, call the auto club, change the tire myself, etc.). Depending on various factors, such as whether I have a spare in good condition, where I need to go and how quickly, or what forms of alternative transportation are available, I would decide on a best course and take action. I would then observe whether or not my actions were effective.

In day-to-day situations, we go through these steps naturally, almost without even thinking about them. However, in situations of very high stress, when our limbic system is active and our frontal lobes are less functional, this natural problem-solving system can break down. It's helpful, therefore, to have a set of steps we can use when we encounter a tough problem. I call this system "1-2-3 check."

1. **Diagnose the problem.** Sometimes we get to work on a solution before we have enough information to identify the real problem. Or we take out our frustration on someone who is not really at fault. The first step is to make observations and determine what's really going on.
2. **Consider possible solutions.** In times of high stress, we are sometimes tempted to do the first thing that comes to mind, which may or may not be the best course of action. This is a brainstorming stage, a time to think of all possible courses of action.
3. **Take the best action.** After considering possible solutions, we should choose the course of action we think will be best, and follow through with it. This is a good time to pray, asking the Holy Spirit for wisdom, to consult with others who can give us guidance, and to consider what has worked in similar situations in the past. In high stress, we can sometimes be overwhelmed with possibilities and become frozen. But there comes a time when we finally must make a decision and act.
4. **Check and see how it worked.** Have you ever known someone to try the same thing again and again, even though it's obviously not working? Popular television psychologist Dr. Phil McGraw observes this at times in families he is talking with, and will ask, "How's that working for you?" We need to pay attention to the results of our problem-solving attempts so that we will know when we should do the same thing again in a similar situation and when we need to come up with something new.

> We don't do our best problem-solving when we are feeling very emotional.

Reflect on a problem you are facing right now, one in which you have some control. Use the steps described here to generate a possible solution.

MY PROBLEM-SOLVING WORKSHEET

What is the problem?

What are my choices?

Which action should I take?

(And later, after you see the results) how did it work?

CHAPTER TWELVE

Problem-Focused Coping, Part Two: Deal Effectively with Conflict

"Blessed are the peacemakers, for they will be called children of God."
— Matthew 5:9 (NAB)

Even when we enter ministry with the best of intentions and try to do our work well, we will sometimes have difficulties working with others. This might be due to personality differences, natural stages in the group process of working together, or it might be because we are encountering a person who thrives on stirring up trouble.

Normal Conflict: Working through Differences in Temperament and Stages of the Group Process

As discussed in Chapter One, we all have different temperaments and personalities, and sometimes different temperament types can conflict with one another. In these instances, it's important to reflect on these natural differences and how they can be gifts to us if we will let them. It is also important to consider the needs of individuals with various temperament types. For example, individuals with a sanguine temperament will need room to dream; individuals with a melancholic temperament will need some details in order to feel comfortable with the plan.

Sometimes difficulties with others might be a result of a group's normal process of learning to work together. Individuals who study group dynamics have identified four stages that groups go through when learning to collaborate:

- In the **forming** stage, group members get to know one another, and tasks and roles are defined.

- In the **storming** stage, personality differences and differences of opinion come out. Group members may argue about various tasks, and sometimes become locked in conflict for a time. It's very important to realize that this is a normal part of learning to work together, and if we can "hang on" during this time, there will be light at the end of the tunnel.

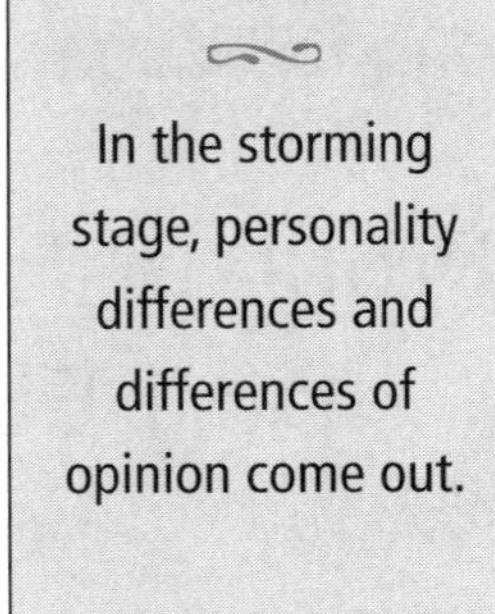

- In the **norming** stage, understandings and compromises are reached, boundaries are defined, and the stage is set for effective work together.
- In the **performing** stage, the group works together. True collaboration exists.

These stages may repeat themselves at times, depending on circumstances and on who else joins the team. New pastors, teachers, or ministry leaders may experience similar stages as a group or parish become accustomed to someone new. In normal conflict situations, it is important to hear others out, show empathy, and practice a spirit of forgiveness and reconciliation.

Abnormal Conflict: Dealing with the Antagonist

Some individuals thrive on conflict and will be present to be a thorn in your side. In his wonderful and much-needed book *Antagonists in the Church*, psychologist Dr. Kenneth Haugk (1988) offers the following questions for identifying whether you might be dealing with an antagonist:

- Is the person's behavior disruptive?
- Is the attack irrational?
- Does the person go out of the way to initiate trouble?
- Are the person's demands insatiable?
- Are the concerns on which the attack is based minimal or fabricated?
- Does the person avoid causes that involve personal risk, suffering, or sacrifice?
- Does the person's motivation appear selfish?

If it becomes apparent that one is dealing with an antagonist, there may be no real solution, other than to set limits. Try to set some boundaries on how much of your time the antagonist is able to consume. Act professionally and courteously, but keep a relative distance.

QUESTIONS FOR REFLECTION

1. What difficulties am I currently having in working with others?

2. Are these difficulties most likely due to ordinary issues such as temperamental differences or group processes, or are they evidence of an antagonist at work in the situation?

3. What is the best course of action at this time?

Putting It All Together

Have no anxiety about anything, but in everything by prayer and supplication with thanksgiving let your requests be made known to God.
— PHILIPPIANS 4:6

Ministry work is an extraordinary responsibility, with eternal consequences. Fortunately, we are not alone when we are working for the Lord. We have brothers and sisters in the Church who are working with us to build God's kingdom, and we have a God who is present with us, guiding us, providing for us, and consoling us when times are hard.

The recommendations in this short book are based on both psychological research and the experience of those in ministry. However, it's important to remember that to be truly effective in ministry work, to work well without becoming overwhelmed or burned out, we must depend on God.

God also calls us to responsibility. We must do our part to work efficiently, cope with stress, and solve problems effectively. He doesn't promise to take our problems away or solve them for us, but He does promise to be present with us as we go about his work: ". . . and lo, I am with you always, to the close of the age" (Mt 28:20).

Prayerfully ask God's help as you work to put these recommendations, and other tools to manage stress, into practice. Try a little at a time, perhaps a chapter each week, and ask God to give you wisdom to find other ways to prevent and manage stress as well. Know that He is with you, and allow yourself to experience His love, grace, and mercy as you minister to His Church. May God bless you for responding to His call.

References

Auerbach, S.M., and S.E. Gramling (1997). *Stress Management Workbook: Techniques and Self-Assessment*. Upper Saddle River, N.J.: Prentice Hall.

Baumeister, R.F., A.M. Stillwell, and S.R. Wotman (1990). "Victim and Perpetrator Accounts of Interpersonal Conflict: Autobiographical Narratives about Anger." *Journal of Personality and Social Psychology* 59:994–1005.

Bennett, A., and L. Bennett (2005). *The Temperament God Gave You*. Manchester, N.H.: Sophia Institute Press.

Cohen, S., and T.A. Wills (1985). "Stress, Social Support, and the Buffering Hypothesis." *Psychological Bulletin*, 98:310–357.

Eisenberg, R., and K. Kelly (1997). *Organize Yourself!* (New and Revised Edition). New York: MacMillan.

Frankl, V.E. (2006). *Man's Search for Meaning*. Boston: Beacon Press.

Haugk, K.C. (1988). *Antagonists in the Church*. Minneapolis: Augsburg Fortress Publishers.

Kendler, K., C.O. Gardner, and C.A. Prescott (1997). "Religion, Psychopathology, and Substance Use and Abuse; a Multimeasure, Genetic-Epidemiologic Study." *American Journal of Psychiatry* 154:322–329.

Mahoney, A., K.I. Pargament, T. Jewell, A.B. Swank, E. Scott, E. Emery, and M. Rye (1999). "Marriage and the Spiritual Realm: The Role of Proximal and Distal Religious Constructs in Marital Functioning." *Journal of Family Psychology* 13:321–338.